Reasons
I Don't Like Being The Baby

Heaven B. Smith

Copyright © 2021 Heaven Smith

All Rights Reserved. No part of this publication may be reproduced or transmitted, stored in a retrieval system, or transmitted in any form or by any means, electronic, mechanical, photocopying, recording, scanning, or otherwise, except as permitted by law, without prior written permission of the author.

Printed in the United States of America
Editor: Sharp Editorial, LLC
Illustrator : Benedicta Buatsie

—Dedication—

First, I dedicate my book to God. "The little child will lead them" (Isaiah 11:6). God blesses me every day when I wake up; He has blessed me with my best friend, Aubrey, and so many other blessings.

Secondly, I dedicate this book to my mom and dad, who support me and cheer me on for every gymnastic competition. My mom and I travel a lot for my competitions. Even when she feels bad from her Multiple Sclerosis (MS), she is still there, and my dad takes care of Aubrey. My sister, Chelsea, is in college, but she attends most of my events as well. Finally, my big brother Derrick. He is currently in the military, serving our country to keep me safe. He cheers me on from a distance. My mom sends him plenty of pictures and videos, holding my medals. I thank God for my family.

Oh, my goodness! I cannot forget my favorite and only auntie Monique! We share birthdays, September 16th. Of course, I also want to dedicate this to my Uncle Johnnie and my cousin Johnnie. I know everyone does not have a family like mine, but I sure wish they did.

My brother and sister are all grown up. My brother went to the army, and my sister left for college. Their bedrooms are empty, the house is quiet, and I miss them a lot.

When I finish my homework on school days, I have no one to play with anymore, no one to laugh with and shout, "I won" as we play games. My parents play with me, but I have more fun with my sister and brother.

Now, with this flu called COVID, we must be extra safe. So, my friends cannot come to my house, and I can't go to their houses, either.

Being the baby is no fun.

With my brother and sister being away, I tell my secrets to my dog, Aubrey. But that is no fun because Aubrey can't talk. She just stares at me and licks my face.

I am full of energy on the weekends, but I have done everything I could do at home. I've tie-dyed T-shirts, did some backflips outside, and baked cookies, too.

There is no one to watch movies with now that my brother and sister are gone. I miss movie nights with candy, cookies, popcorn, and all the yummy stuff you can think of eating. After a scary movie,
I would cuddle with my sister, which made me feel a lot better.

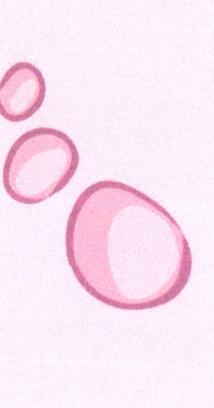

Without my brother and sister, I have no one to run up and down the stairs with me. There is no one to help me eat the veggies off my plate, especially the peas. Yuck! There is no one to climb into bed with when I am lonely. Mom and Dad snore so loud!

But, as the baby, I enjoy some awesome things that my sister and brother miss, like hugs and kisses from Mom. Oh, and enjoying yummy meals at home, too! Dad is learning to cook special recipes, so he and Mom make delicious meals together.

When I think about being the baby, maybe it is not so bad. Being the baby means I have Mom and Dad all to myself. I have a big brother and a big sister that I love and a happy home to call my own..

I have some crazy fears. Do you have fears? I am afraid of all bugs! Spiders, mosquitos, and if I see roach, I will almost pass out. Shots and bullies are the worst!

Let's share. Write down some of your fears.

_____
_____
_____
_____
_____
_____
_____
_____
_____
_____
_____

Three of my favorite things are candy, soda, fun places like the trampoline park and food places. Whoops, I added four.

What are your favorite four things?

I have things I don't like as a kid. I don't like Halloween. It's scary. Sometimes I don't like school. Kids are really mean, and fighting is wrong. I don't like getting bad grades.

Tell me some things you don't like!

Ok our last one. Adults say we shouldn't worry, but I am human. I see things.

I worry about my brother, because he is an African America male, and I don't want him to get hurt. Shhh, the adults can't know our secret. We worry.

I worry one day my dog will die, because she's old. She has been with me all my life.

I worry about the house catching on fire when I try to cook.

Enough about me. I can go all day. Tell me some things you are worried about. It's ok, it's me Heaven.

Doesn't it feel good to share? Whew, I feel better. I hope you do too. If you ever need to share, a diary is a good place to start. Thank you for sharing with me!
Heaven!